SALLY THE MOOSE

AUTHORED AND ILLUSTRATED BY
GIANNA RITZ-VENNELL

Gianna Ritz-Vennell

Her heart feels loved and truly blessed.
This is her story, truth be told.

Sally the moose loves to eat flowers; white daisies that grow in May!

She watches the rain as it showers.
"The sky is turning gray."

Sally the moose plays down the stream, before resting her hooves in the sun.

She falls asleep and has a dream
of her day filled with laughter and fun.

Sally the moose discovered a tree
so big it touches the sky.

"This is a maple tree," says the bee.
"A yummy fall treat you must try!"

Sally the moose enjoys the snow,
while rolling around in a cloud of white.

The mountain range shines with a glow.
She looks at the moon and whispers,
"goodnight."

Sally the moose loves to ski.
Down the mountain she goes!

After the race, she drinks some tea, before her tiny hooves froze.

Sally the moose watches the seasons change.
"Each one is unique, I love them all."

Her heart feels loved and truly blessed.
This is her story, truth be told.

The End.

"This book is dedicated to the beautiful town of Stowe, Vermont. While visiting Stowe in 2018, my husband and I witnessed a female moose grazing off the side of the road. She was a beautiful creature. At that time, "Sally the Moose" came to mind. I wanted to share my love for Vermont in a creative way!"
-Gianna Ritz-Vennell

ABOUT THE AUTHOR/ILLUSTRATOR

-Gianna lives in New Jersey, where she likes to visit the beach and local farmers markets.

-Gianna loves road-tripping to Stowe, Vermont with her husband, Frank and their dogs, Briar and Dolly.

-Gianna is an art teacher in the same school that she attended as a little girl.

Sally the Moose Word Search

M	A	N	S	F	I	E	L	D	H	V	P	S	R
E	S	K	I	A	S	N	O	W	F	L	A	K	E
N	M	N	S	E	R	U	T	N	E	V	D	A	T
N	A	V	E	R	M	O	N	T	E	I	S	V	A
T	A	A	W	O	N	O	O	M	M	M	Y	R	S
S	N	O	W	U	E	H	C	T	O	R	R	E	G
M	L	R	O	E	O	M	A	R	O	E	U	E	M
S	C	W	I	R	E	D	M	E	S	M	P	B	O
T	H	I	Y	T	S	O	D	E	E	E	I	A	N
O	E	N	L	P	A	I	N	T	I	N	G	N	O
W	E	T	L	M	A	P	L	E	E	W	A	E	R
E	S	E	A	M	O	U	N	T	A	I	N	T	A
E	E	R	S	H	O	O	V	E	S	T	M	P	N
U	L	E	S	T	R	E	A	M	E	O	M	S	N

PAINTING
ADVENTURE
STREAM
MOOSE
VERMONT
SALLY
MOON
BEE
TREE
MANSFIELD
SNOWFLAKE
MOUNTAIN
WINTER
SNOW
SYRUP
SKI
CHEESE
HOOVES
MAPLE
STOWE

Design Sally's bow!

On this page, draw a picture of your favorite place to visit!

Made in the USA
Columbia, SC
28 January 2020